# ADVENTURES IN COLONIAL AMERICA

# JAMESTOWN

## New World Adventure

by James E. Knight

illustrated by David Wenzel

W9-AWJ-314

Troll

*Cover art by Shi Chen.*

Copyright © 1982 by Troll Communications L.L.C.

All rights reserved. No part of this book may be reproduced or utilized in any form or by any means, electronic or mechanical, including photocopying, recording, or by any information storage and retrieval system, without written permission from the publisher.

This edition published 1998 by Troll Communications L.L.C.

Printed in the United States of America.

10   9

*Library of Congress Cataloging-in-Publication Data*

Knight, James E.
  Jamestown, New World adventure.

  Summary: Two English children are told the story of their grandfather's experiences as one of the original Jamestown colonists of 1607.
    1. Jamestown (Va.)—History—Juvenile literature.
[1. Jamestown (Va.)—History.  2. United States—History—Colonial period, ca. 1600–1775.]  I. Wenzel,
David, 1950–     ill.   II. Title.
F234.J3K64     973.2'1     81-23086
ISBN 0-89375-724-1     AACR2
ISBN 0-8167-4554-4 (pbk.)

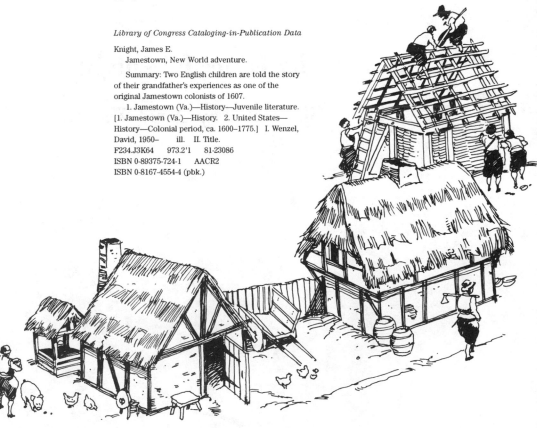

# JAMESTOWN

## New World
## Adventure

The fire crackled and danced on the hearth. Julia Redfield looked at her son and daughter. They were seated on the floor, warming their feet before the flames.

"Are you ready to hear the story of your grandfather's time in America?" she asked.

They both nodded. "Is that Grandfather Worth's journal?" Benjamin asked.

"Yes, I've saved it for a long time. Now you are both old enough to understand what it says."

"Father told me that the Indians burned down the James Towne settlement two years ago," Lydia said.

"I know," said her mother. "Times have been hard for that little colony in the Virginia wilderness. But it was even worse in your grandfather's time."

"Read to us, Mother," Benjamin said. "I want to hear what happened."

Julia Redfield opened the worn and yellowed pages of the journal. She began to read.

*May 14, 1607*

This journal will record the adventures of Israel Worth in the new colony of James Towne. At the time of this first entry, I am twenty-eight years old and in good health. I am one of four master carpenters on this expedition.

As I write, I am aboard the ship *Susan Constant*, with Captain Christopher Newport in command. Two other ships are also anchored in this pleasant bay. They are the *Godspeed* and the *Discovery*.

I will write as often as I am able. For I know that we will all be laboring hard for this new colony of the Virginia Company, and time will be scarce.

How sweet the land smells after our long voyage. From the ship I can see a white sandy beach and tall pines. The air is mild. The river beyond this bay looks broader than any I have seen in England. As with our colony, the river has been named James, after our King.

When we entered the Bay of the Chesapeake, a few days back, there was trouble. We were anchored off a point of land, which the Captain called Cape Henry. He and some of our men went ashore. They were attacked by Indians. Two sailors were wounded by arrows, and one of them died today.

Earlier today we carried men and goods to shore. Some of the men are now asleep in canvas shelters in the forest. I will go ashore tomorrow.

When we arrived in this wilderness, Captain Newport opened a sealed box he had brought from the Virginia Company in England. It contained the names of the seven men who will be our Councilors, or leaders, here. One of the names was that of Captain John Smith. I, for one, was surprised by this choice. Captain Smith had been under arrest for some time on the voyage over. I know not why. The other leaders do not seem to like him. But he has taken the Councilors' oath of office along with the rest.

*June 7*

For three weeks now, I have been ashore. We are clearing the land. From dawn to dusk we labor at cutting down trees.

Despite our earlier troubles with the Indians, things had been going smoothly between us. We have seen them several times, and they have given us corn.

But yesterday, while some of our leaders were out exploring, trouble began. Some two hundred warriors attacked with spears and arrows. Many of us were wounded, and one boy was killed. We drove the Indians back with musketfire. They seem terrified of it.

This has taught us a hard lesson. We must build a fort to protect ourselves. We will call it James Fort, and it will face the river. As a carpenter, I will be busy with this for some time. The fort will be made of upright logs, and it will be shaped like a triangle. Other buildings will be added later. Bulwarks will be erected at each corner of the fort. From these high towers, we will set up our artillery.

9

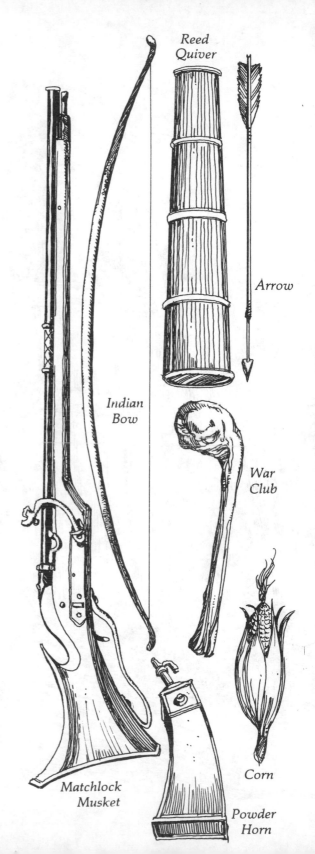

Reed Quiver

Arrow

Indian Bow

War Club

Matchlock Musket

Corn

Powder Horn

*June 23*

We have worked hard these past weeks in warm temperatures. We must try to settle this colony as soon as possible for the Virginia Company. Yesterday Captain Newport sailed for England on the *Susan Constant*. The *Godspeed* sailed, too. Now we are but one hundred souls alone on this foreign shore.

Yet, we are too busy to be lonely or afraid. James Fort is nearly finished, and it is very handsome. I am proud of having built the West Bulwark with my own hands. We have planted a wheat field beside the fort. As a carpenter, I have much to do here. I have helped to build our chapel, too, and other buildings.

"Grandfather Worth must have been very skilled," said Lydia.

"Indeed, he was," said her mother, "as were many others on the expedition. But not all of them, unfortunately. Your grandfather records that some of them were 'gentlemen.' They would not work with their hands. While your grandfather and the others worked, they sat about or went off in search of gold."

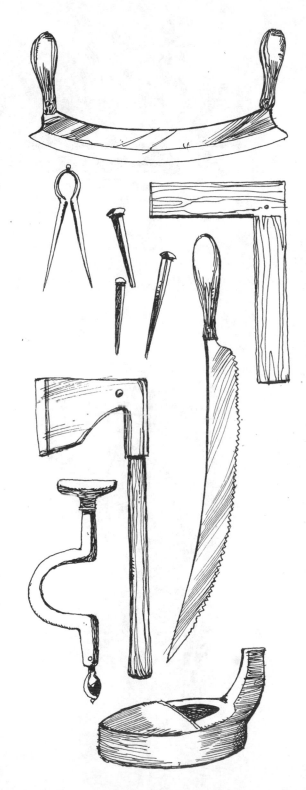

"Why didn't the others make the gentlemen work?" Lydia asked.

"I don't know," her mother said. "However, your grandfather writes that Captain Wingfield, who was elected the Council president for a year, did nothing about it. Captain John Smith thought this was foolhardy. He said the colony could not survive without storing food for winter and building shelters. Captain Smith believed the men should not be wasting time looking for gold, even if that is what the Virginia Company wanted."

"What happened next?" asked Benjamin.

Mrs. Redfield began reading again.

*July 5*

Sudden disease has struck our colony. Ten days ago we were in good health. Now men take to their beds, shaking with fever. They die—of what we often do not know. We bury them secretly at night. We are afraid that the Indians will learn how few we are.

Captain Smith is not surprised by the disease. He says that we should have dug freshwater wells. Instead, we have been drinking from the bay at low tide, when the water is least salty.

The Captain says this disease is caused by hot weather, hard work, and bad diet.

How strange that our food supplies should be low. We are on half-rations now. Yet, this land is not without plenty. Birds and fur-bearing animals fill the forest. Raccoons grow large as foxes. Crabs, mussels, oysters, and fish are plentiful. But we do not have the skills of the Indians. We cannot catch enough fish or hunt enough animals to feed ourselves.

The wheat we planted does not grow well. The meat we brought with us and our biscuits are gone. We sometimes barter with the Indians for corn—but it is not enough. We eat the barley and wheat that is left from our voyage. They are wormy from weeks at sea.

Despite our misery, the gentlemen still go forth on their gold-seeking parties. I agree with Captain Smith. What foolishness this is!

*September 5*

Half our number—over fifty souls—are dead and buried. Sadness and fear have taken over the colony. One of our seven Councilors is dead. Other men have been killed by the arrows of unfriendly Indians. One man was executed for speaking treason against the Crown.

But most have died of disease and starvation. I go to my bed hungry each night. Tonight I have a few kernels of corn in my stomach. And so I am lucky. I will probably awake in the morning.

*October 13*

Three of the gold-seekers were killed yesterday by Indians of the Pamunkey Nation. They are part of the much-feared chiefdom of King Powhatan.

Our canvas tents are rotting away. Now we are building cabins with thatched roofs supported on posts. The walls are woven with hazel or willow branches and then plastered with mud. We have learned from the Indians' wigwams. We leave a hole in the roof through which smoke can escape.

"How did they ever get through the winter?" Benjamin asked. "Father says it grows very cold in Virginia."

"Yes," said his mother. "The colony suffered from frostbite and illness. And there was so little to eat. Everyone began to see that Captain Wingfield was not fit to lead the colony. More and more, your grandfather and others began to listen to Captain Smith. Then, in December, your grandfather writes that Captain Smith and nine other men left on an expedition to explore the Chickahominy River."

"What happened?" Lydia asked.

"In the entry for December 24, the Captain had still not returned. But a friendly Indian told the colonists that Smith had been taken prisoner."

"Was that true?" asked Benjamin.

"Let me read what is written here," replied his mother.

*January 1, 1608*

Praise be! The Captain has returned with the New Year! He was indeed a prisoner of Chief Powhatan. But he was treated well. And now he speaks of a new time of peace and friendliness with the Indians.

But the other Councilors are jealous of this man. Now they talk of hanging him because two men were killed on the expedition.

*January 4*

All talk of hanging has been forgotten. Our old ship the *Susan Constant* has returned from England! It sailed into the bay two days ago with one hundred new settlers and supplies. How happy we were to see them!

Along with the supplies, there was eagerly awaited mail. I received a long letter from my dear wife with

16

news of our young daughter. There was great merry-making in James Towne on that day.

"You must have been very young then, Mother," said Lydia.

Mrs. Redfield smiled. "Young, indeed," she said. "But my poor father. No sooner had he received news from home than tragedy struck again. His entry for January 7 records a fire in the fort. Many of the cabins were burned. Old and new settlers were greatly discouraged. There was talk of going home. But once again the Indians helped them. Listen."

*February 28*

Much has happened. We shall not leave James Towne after all. Captain Smith's new friends among Powhatan's people have saved us. They come out of the forest often now. They bring fish, bread, corn, turkeys, and raccoons. Without them, we would never survive.

A young Indian maiden often leads the food-bearers. She is Pocahontas, daughter of King Powhatan and a Princess in this land. I cannot but think she is only eleven or twelve years of age. But she has shown herself to be a true friend.

"Didn't Pocahontas come to London a few years after that?" Benjamin asked.

"Yes," said his mother. "She married an Englishman, John Rolfe, and they visited London in 1616. She was presented to the Court, and everyone was charmed by her. But, sadly, she died of smallpox while still in England. But, listen, your grandfather writes more of her."

*April 20*

Pocahontas comes almost every other day. She and the other Indians bring food to us. And she carries messages back and forth between her father and Captain Smith. More and more, many of us feel that the Captain should be our leader.

Ten days ago, the *Susan Constant* sailed again for England. And today, the *Phoenix* sailed into our bay. Once again, we have more settlers.

*May 14*

James Towne is one year old today! It is longer than that since I have seen my home and family. My old friend, Angus Murchison, and I are sad. We are among the few "old men" in this place. There are but thirty-eight of us left from the original one hundred.

There has been Indian trouble once more. They have taken tools, spades, hatchets, and other things. Captain Smith was greatly angered, and he took several Indians as hostages.

But, once more, Pocahontas saved us. She arrived with presents and food from Powhatan, her father. He sent his word that his people will give us no more trouble.

*June 2*

This day Captain Smith and fourteen men left James Towne on a barge. The Captain means to explore and map the entire Bay of the Chesapeake. I wished to go with him, but I was told I am needed here. And so I stay.

*July 12*

Captain Smith is still away. We pray for his safe return. Our corn has ripened in the summer sun. Now we have fresh kernels to eat. But I wonder if we have stored enough for the winter months. And sometimes I wonder if I will ever see my wife and child again.

"Did Captain Smith come back, Mother?" Lydia asked.

"Yes, your grandfather writes that on September 7, the Captain and his men returned. Everyone thought things would be better then."

"And were they?" asked Benjamin.

"For a time, yes," said his mother. "Your grandfather was very happy when Captain Smith was at last elected president of the Council. And on September 20, eighty new settlers arrived, including the first two women. But the Virginia Company had not sent the blacksmiths and farmers and carpenters who were needed. Instead, they had sent glassmakers and gold refiners."

"Did they find gold?" Lydia asked.

In reply, her mother read again from the journal.

*December 10*

For a week we have been splitting logs and loading them aboard the ship. Today it set sail for England. We must send something back to the Virginia Company in London—even if it is only wood for roofing. There is no gold to be found here.

Captain Smith has taken charge and has done much. The fort has been made larger and stronger. A storehouse and other buildings have been added. We have dug a well.

The Captain instructs us in military drill. He says we must be prepared to defend ourselves. Each Saturday, he parades us on the field by the West Bulwark. Then we blast away at tree stumps with our muskets for target practice. The Indians watch in amazement.

Captain Smith may be strict, but he is fair. A few grumble, but we respect him. Everybody must work at some useful task. He has laid down the law to the gentlemen, too. Those who do not work do not eat, he says.

*January 30, 1609*

It is winter again, and a New Year. The colony has lasted through these cruel months only because of Captain Smith. When our food runs low, he goes to Powhatan. He gets corn and other goods from him.

*March 18*

I have no English ink left for my quill. However, I prepare a brownish broth of dried berries. It serves well enough, and it does not fade.

Princess Pocahontas still visits us often. She teaches
us the way her people fish and plant corn. Her laughter
is merry to hear. Captain Smith, like all of us, is very
fond of her.

*June 28*

We face starvation once more. Rats infest our storehouse of corn. We had counted on this supply of food to last until the autumn harvest ripens. Some men have been sent to Point Comfort to fish. Some have gone downstream to catch oysters.

*July 22*

It is very hot. Disease has broken out again. The men grow lazy and discouraged. They refuse to work or gather food. But the Captain will not allow this. Truly, he keeps our colony together with his great will and strength.

## August 12

Yesterday six ships anchored at James Towne! They were battered and weather-beaten. They are part of a large relief supply sent by the Virginia Company. Unfortunately, the flagship, the *Sea Venture*, was blown off course near Bermuda. Some fear the *Sea Venture*'s passengers are lost forever.

The ships that did arrive brought three hundred new settlers. Surely we need them, but we have not so much as a roof to cover their heads. And they are ill-prepared for life here. How shall we feed them when winter comes?

## August 30

People are taking sides for or against Captain Smith. We "old men" know we owe him our lives. So we will never desert him. Surely this colony could not survive without him.

*September 3*

Captain Smith has been injured. While he was out on the barge, his powder bag exploded. The men carried him back to the fort more dead than alive. We pray for his recovery.

*October 3*

Today, Captain Smith was taken aboard one of the ships. He must sail for England. He has no other choice. With his painful injuries, he cannot carry on.

But how shall we survive without him?

"What happened then?" asked Benjamin.

"Listen to what your grandfather writes," replied his mother. She turned a page in the journal and began reading.

*November 16*

Things are worse in James Towne, now that Captain Smith is gone. Food is scarce. Some of the new settlers have already died. Our leaders fight among themselves. No one leads.

There is no one to deal with Powhatan and his people. Our leaders are cruel to the Indians. So they turn against us. They bring no more food. They attack us in the forest. They know that Smith has gone. And Pocahontas comes no more.

*January 4, 1610*

Midwinter. We are starving to death. Men will do anything for food. They eat any living thing—dogs, cats, snakes, mice. When these are gone, they eat leather and clothing. Some wander into the forest and are killed by Indians. Some go off to live with the Indians. They are never seen again.

The dead are the fortunate ones. Their suffering is over.

28

*February 25*

This is truly the starving time. I can hardly stand from weakness. When Captain Smith departed, there were five hundred of us. There are, I think, but one hundred left now.

For food today, I found some young hazel logs. I stripped away the green bark and chewed it for the juices.

My wife and daughter are much in my thoughts. God bless them and keep them. And God help me.

Julia Redfield stopped reading for a moment. The children were silent. Then Lydia asked, "What happened to Grandfather? I know that he did not come back to England."

"No, your grandfather did not leave the colony," said Mrs. Redfield. "Here, I will read the final entry."

And she turned to the last yellowed page in the journal.

*May 11, 1610*

I feel I must write these last words in this record. This is not the hand of Israel Worth. It is his good friend, Angus Murchison. The time of the great starving is past. But Israel did not survive. Two days after he last put his quill to paper, he left the fort with some others to search for food. They never returned.

The loss of Israel has saddened us all. He always labored hard. He did not complain. Gentlemen and commoners alike respected him. You may be proud of that. James Towne could not have survived without men like Israel Worth.

And James Towne *has* survived. New settlers and supplies have arrived. We who are left are but a few scarecrows. But we will try again. And we will succeed.

I will see that these papers reach Israel's wife in England.

*God save and keep our colony.*

"I think Grandfather Worth was a very brave man," said Lydia.

"I think perhaps they all were," said Benjamin.

# Index